Junk

'Melvin Burgess is a writer of the highest quality with exceptional powers of insight' *The Sunday Tmes*

'John Retallack's excellent adaptation of Melvin Burgess's controversial Carnegie Medal winning novel is splendidly unpatronising . . . a truly cautionary tale' *Independent*

'Junk is perhaps the clearest sign yet that British theatre for children and young people is beginning to grow up' *Guardian*

Melvin Burgess was born in London in 1954 and was brought up in Sussex and Surrey. After leaving school at eighteen he began training as a journalist. He then had occasional jobs, mainly in the building industry. He started writing in his twenties and wrote on and off for fifteen years before having his first book *The Cry of the Wolf* accepted for publication by Andersen Press in 1990. He is now regarded as one of the best writers in contemporary children's literature. Burgess's books are not always easy; dealing with tough subjects such as homelessness, disability, child abuse, witchcraft and drugs. *Junk* won both the Carnegie Medal and the Guardian Children's Fiction Prize. He now writes full time and lives in Lancashire. He has two children, Oliver and Pearl.

John Retallack has directed many new plays for young audiences, including Ad Bont's *Mirad, Boy from Bosnia* (1993/4) and Niklas Radström's *Hitler's Childhood* (1994). He has directed two of Renata Allen's award-winning plays for children, including *The Magic Storybook* (1992). His own adaptations include Cervantes' *Don Quixote*, Robert Musil's *Man Without Qualities*, Alfred Jarry's *Ubu Roi*, Bryon's *Don Juan*, Italo Calvino's *Italian Folk Tales* and Dario Fo's *Mistero Buffo*. For the last eighteen years he ran two touring companies, Oxford Stage Company and Actors' Touring Company (ATC). His productions for these companies have been seen throughout the UK and in over thirty countries abroad. He is currently setting up a new theatre company for young people called Company of Angels. He now lives in London with Renata Allen and their two children Hanna and Jack.

Published by Methuen 1999

1 3 5 7 9 10 8 6 4 2

First published in Great Britain in 1999
by Methuen Publishing Limited
215 Vauxhall Bridge Road, London, SW1V 1EJ

Peribo Pty Limited, 58 Beaumont Road, Mount Kuring-Gai,
NSW 2080, Australia, ACN 002 273 761
(for Australia and New Zealand)

Methuen Publishing Limited Reg. No. 3543167

A CIP catalogue record for this book is available from the British Library

100155466l   ISBN 0 413 73840 X   T

Typeset by SX Composing DTP, Rayleigh, Essex
Printed and bound in Great Britain
by Cox & Wyman Ltd, Reading, Berkshire

Caution

JUNK

by **Melvin Burgess**

adapted for the stage by **John Retallack**

Methuen Drama

Introduction

Looking back to the summer of 1997, when *Junk* won the Carnegie Medal and provoked a small blizzard of controversy in the media, the thing that strikes me most is the lack of controversy I've come across over it ever since. All the debate about the innocence of childhood – the high-minded opinions about how children shouldn't read such depressing stuff and how young minds shouldn't be exposed to something so potentially corrupting as an authentic account of addiction – seems to have turned, overnight, into universal approval. I've not come across a single complaint since. *Junk* the book, and the play, has been taken up by teachers, who regard it as having both appeal and literary merit; by drug educationalists, who find it a useful and rare resource to work with – a story that presents a picture of real people making real decisions in real situations – by young people; and by teenagers, who like it because . . .

Well, why do they like it? When I visit schools it's always *Junk* they want me to talk about, always *Junk* that has currency in the classrooms and corridors. Traditionally, books for teenagers don't sell, and as a children's writer you are endlessly reminded that if you want your royalties to go up, the age of your readership has to go down. *Junk* could have crashed – for a while I seriously considered trying to get it published as an adult novel for that reason. I don't think anyone foresaw the reaction or the success that awaited it. The aim in writing the book was a simple one: to write a novel about drug culture that told it how it was. It had to be authentic, it had to be told with unflinching honesty and, most of all, with an explicit trust in a young audience to be able to assimilate it. I had nothing to teach, no point of view to peddle. If the novel was authentic people could and would draw their own conclusions without any help from me. I think it paid off for two reasons. One is that authenticity makes for good books, whatever age group you're writing for. The other, of course, is that people habitually and consistently underestimate a teenage audience.

Junk taught me that a teenage audience is as sophisticated as you care to treat it. Fiction, or theatre, or television for this age group has to compete directly with material presented to adults. We all know that teenagers aged fourteen and younger watch pretty much whatever is showing . . . why should we think that they'll put up with anything less in material presented directly to them? We live in an age with no secrets. Television, and now the Internet, has put paid to that. The traditional ways of letting young people learn by leaving them to eavesdrop on our grown-up conversations has been happening on a grand scale in the past ten years. If there is to be proper fiction for teenagers it must credit them fully with what they already know.

There has always been a great deal of disrespect for teenagers, a feeling that you can't be straight with them for fear of what they might do . . . or is it a fear of what their parents might say? Either way, this has led to a tendency in fiction, despite its increasing desire to deal with difficult issues, to treat teenagers in a very grown-up, responsible way. What's wrong with that? Well, nothing; but what about that other type of fiction, the private kind? The sort of book which you open up and think . . . I know these people, I know what they're doing . . . it's just like me. It's a kind of fiction that talks to you about yourself not just as a mature, responsible adult, but as someone who doesn't always do the right thing. I wanted *Junk* to be a book not for people who were about to do the responsible thing, but for those who were about to do the irresponsible thing – that is, at some time or another, for all of us. Statistically, it is said that eighty per cent of people try out drugs in some way or other before they reach twenty. Not very responsible of course; but somehow, very few of them end up having problems of addiction.

I've certainly nothing against people learning things from novels, but I do feel that one of the reasons for *Junk*'s success was that the novel allowed the reader to approach it in their own way and to take from it what they chose to take. OK, it's a book about heroin addiction, and you'd have to be very extreme to approve of that, but at least it allows you to understand how such a thing can happen, and happen to someone maybe not so very different from yourself, without insisting on pushing advice about how to avoid it. Not so much a question of being unpatronising, but of trusting a young readership to place the book in the context of their own experience in a realistic way.

I know John Retallack had the same aims in mind with his stage adaptation. He draws both the celebratory side of drugs and the downs with a clear line, and I'm delighted to see my story represented in the threatre by this play.

Melvin Burgess, December 1998

Melvin Brugess's novel *Junk* shocked many moral commentators due to its graphic descriptions of underage sex, hard drug abuse and prostitution. Its depiction of two fourteen-year-old heroin addicts and their slide away from 'civilised' life, its playful subversive passages, such as 'Gemma Brogan's practical handbook to running away from home', and the gluing up of banks (the latter a particular favourite when Melvin has read passages in schools) were seen by some as too shocking for young people's literature. This kind of moralistic attitude is also widespread in much theatre for young people, forgetting the fact that most young teenagers are exposed to certificate eighteen films, pornography and so on. Sexual openness and the accessibility of drugs are part of our teenage culture, and have been for many years. *Junk* the stage play aims to celebrate the energy of a lifestyle that embraces drugs and sex and then to chart the horrifying consequences of addiction, especially in the way it destroys the youthfulness of the takers whose very energy and curiosity led them to drugs in the first place.

Junk is completely without cynicism. It is first and foremost a love story, an adventure underscored by the wild sounds of the late seventies and early eighties, a celebration of nonconformist youth culture emerging from punk and other alternative lifestyles. Indeed, the idea of punk, which is to do everything your parents told you not to: dress in the dirtiest, most destroyed clothes, have lots of sex, experiment with drugs, pierce your body, don't go to work or school (in Lily's terms, 'the straights . . . going to learn how to go to work'), underpins the whole of the play. It is brutal and unsentimental, charting with enormous speed the lives of kids who want to leave their families but find themselves merely setting up alternative families for themselves; having babies, splitting up, so that a normal cycle of, say, ten years is collapsed into four. By the end of *Junk* Gemma is not the wild punk rejecting all family ties but the reverse, as Vonny comments: 'an old, old woman telling me what had happened to her when she was still young.' Her own mother summarises when she says: 'My first thought was, My God, she looks like my mother . . . my own mother. An old woman.'

As we have worked on *Junk* we have all become aware of this huge counter-culture associated with heroin, into which we can only leap imaginatively. John Retallack asks the actors to imagine they are having an imaginary 'phantom affair' with the drug. The more we research and the more we rehearse, the more heroin is revealed as a kind of perfect partner, offering unconditional love.

It is seen as the all-powerful, multi-purpose drug, giving an overwhelming feeling of peace to its users, wrapping them in cotton wool to insulate them from any problems. Tar seems drawn to it because of his overwhelming family problems and perhaps that is why he remains an addict. To come down is to have to confront those initial problems you ran away from which come back at you with renewed force.

Theatrically, nothing would have been more boring than spending two hours watching junkies getting their hit on stage. This is because the heroin high, the feeling of euphoria, is very much an internal thing, and a junkie experiencing the equivalent of ultimate pleasure may be looking thoroughly miserable from the outside and will often be 'on the nod'; nodding in and out of sleep and wakefulness. Not, in fact, very dramatic. So, partly we have structured the play so that right until well into the second act we celebrate the pleasure of taking the drug in the early stages. We have also focused on showing the characters at the dramatic high points when the drug brings them into conflict with reality. Key points would be the crisis, during the walk they take, when they realise they can't get off it, the fury of Lily, paranoid to the point of distraction, when she sees Gemma's hand on her baby, or her anger at being told she has to abort her baby because she's a junkie. Indeed, the self-deception of the characters is a means by which they become distanced from us, clearly occupying a different world: Tar's 'It doesn't mean I haven't given up', or Lily's 'I can give up any time I want' show us how far the drug has taken them from knowing themselves.

The actors and many of the production team were roughly the same age as Gemma and Tar in the early eighties. It has been a curious mixture of a journey into an unknown drug's landscape, as well as a journey to familiar territory with the music of The Clash, The Cure, The Buzzcocks, New Order, Ian Dury, and all the memories they bring back of early teenage years. The technique of presentation has been rather like those album covers of punk bands with torn paper edges: we rip straight into scenes at, or just before, the dramatic high point so that we don't have to set up each scene with a beginning, middle and end. We hope that this style is true to the spirit of punk, and the sudden experience of taking smack itself; pushing down the plunger to change, immediately, your whole state of body and mind.

John Retallack and Ben Harrison, October 1998

Junk

Junk was first produced by Oxford Stage Company. It opened at The Castle, Wellingborough, on 15 January 1998, with the following cast:

Tar	Dan Rosewarne
Gemma Brogan	Emma Rydal
Mrs Brogan	Charlotte Fields
Mr Brogan	James Traherne
Richard	Matthew Cureton
Vonny	Tracy Sweetinburgh
Jerry	James Traherne
Tar's mum	Tracy Sweetinburgh
Lily	Paula Bacon
Rob	James Traherne
Sal	Charlotte Fields
Steve	Matthew Cureton
Barry	Matthew Cureton
Policeman	James Traherne
Policewoman	Tracy Sweetinburgh

Director: John Retallack
Composer / Sound Designer: Karl James
Designer: Niki Turner
Lighting Designer: Bruno Poet
Assistant Director: Ben Harrison
Production Manager: Katrina Gilroy
Company Manager: Sid Charlton
Deputy Stage Manager: Chris Marcus
Assistant Stage Manager: Abi Duddlestone
Wardrobe Mistress: Debee Lane

Act One

Scene One

Gemma, **Tar**, **Barry**.

Low light – **Gemma** *and* **Tar** *in the back seat of a family car, in a garage.*

Gemma   I'm hungry.

Tar *turns on torch and looks in rucksack.*

Tar   There's an apple.

Gemma   Nah. Any crisps left?

Tar   Nope.

Gemma   It's blooming cold in this garage.

Tar   Barry'll be here soon. Sorry you came?

Gemma   Nah. You better save the batteries.

Tar *switches off the torch.*

Tar   Come with me.

Gemma   What? You must be crazy.

Tar   Why not?

Gemma   What have I got to run away from?

Tar   Oh come on, it'd be something to do. You're always saying how bored you are.

Gemma   That's true. I go dizzy with boredom here. Still . . . what about school and that?

Tar   You can go to school any time.

Gemma   I can run away any time in my life, Tar. I'm sorry.

Noise from behind them.

Barry It's only me . . . .

Gemma Bloody hell – you nearly killed me.

Barry Sorry. Here, switch that torch on so's I can see where I'm going . . . .

Tar *switches on torch.*

Barry I suppose we ought to have a secret knock or something. Here . . . (*Hands over a bag.*) It's only rolls and cheese. They'd have missed anything else.

Gemma Didn't you get any butter?

Barry No. But I did get some pickle.

Gemma Branston. Brilliant!

Gemma *begins tearing up the rolls and chunks of cheese, she spreads the pickle with her finger.*

Barry Christ he really laid into you this time, didn't he?

Gemma Looks like a bowl of rotten fruit, doesn't it? Not that you'd want to eat it . . . .

Barry You haven't been turning the light on, by the way, have you? Only . . . .

Gemma We said we wouldn't, didn't we?

Barry . . . Only they might see it through the cracks in the garage door.

Gemma I told you . . . .

Barry All right.

Gemma *stuffs a roll into her mouth.*

Gemma Wan won?

Tar Yeah please . . . .

Barry When are you going?

Tar   Tomorrow.

Barry   Got everything?

Tar *pats his rucksack.*

Barry   But what about your mum?

Gemma   His mum's gonna be all right. She'll probably clear off herself once Tar's gone. She's only been staying because of him anyway; she's said that thousands of times, hasn't she?

Barry   Right. Best thing you could do for her, clear off. She won't have anything to tie her to the old bastard then.

Tar   That's what I'm hoping.

Barry *lingers;* **Tar** *makes faces at him to go. Exit* **Barry**. *Pause. A noise of bodies moving in the dark.*

Tar   Come 'ere you, come 'ere . . .

Gemma   Naughty . . .

Tar   Why not?

Gemma   Not here, not in Barry's garage. I just don't want it to go any further.

Tar   You might never see me again after tonight.

Gemma   No. I said no.

Tar   It won't go any further then.

Gemma   Good.

They sleep. Lights up on **Gemma** *and* **Tar**. **Gemma** *is still asleep in* **Tar**'s *arms. It is dawn.*

Tar (*to audience*)   My name is David. But Gemma calls me Tar, because I always say to her 'Stop smoking or you'll get tar in your lungs.' I'm off. I'm leaving Minely-on-Sea and I'm off to Bristol. My dad beat me up yesterday. It wasn't the first time. Why did he do that? Because I cleaned the house. And my mum? She's too pissed to do it. He was going on at her for using me like a skivvy, and she was screaming at him for getting between her and her son. I couldn't win either way. So I'm off. I'm off to Bristol.

Exit **Tar** *with bag.*

Gemma (*to audience*)   Last night in the garage, we never did anything. I mean, I wanted to sleep with him. It would have been a nice way to say goodbye, and poor Tar could have done with that. That's to say, if I'd done it before, it would have been a nice way to say goodbye. I only didn't do it for my parents. I wanted to be able to say, look, this was my boyfriend. He was in some really nasty trouble, he'd been beat up by his dad for the nth time, he was running away and I spent the night with him because he needed some company. And I think he might be in love with me. It was just . . . being close. Now is that human or what? The only thing I regret is that I put my dad before Tar. I won't make that mistake twice.

Scene Two

Gemma, **Mr Brogan** (**Gemma**'s *dad*), **Mrs Brogan** (**Gemma**'s *mum*).

Mrs Brogan   Your father's right Gemma, there have to be rules. Surely you can see that?

Gemma   Look . . . Tar was upset. He just needed someone to stay with him. But there was no sex. Honest. All right?

Pause.

Mr Brogan   Liar.

Gemma *exits to her bedroom, slamming doors.*

Gemma   Just . . . drop down dead!
(*To audience.*) I locked myself in my room and tried to take the planet over with music.

Cyndi Lauper, 'Girls Just Wanna Have Fun' plays, **Gemma** *dances.*

Mr Brogan *enters the room and switches the music off.*

Mr Brogan   I'm sorry Gemma I shouldn't have said that.

Gemma   I'm sorry too. You're still my number one daddy.

Enter **Mrs Brogan**.

Mrs Brogan   Have you two made friends now?

Mr Brogan   Oh, yes. Er, we were just discussing what to do next, weren't we, Gemma?

Mrs Brogan *puts her arm in* **Mr Brogan**'*s arm.*

Mrs Brogan   Now you are going to have to do as we say in future, Gemma.

Gemma   Yes, Mum.

Mrs Brogan   You're not going out in the week; me or your father will inspect your homework every evening. And you are forbidden to see David.

Mr Brogan   Or those louts that hang out by the seafront.

Mrs Brogan   Your other privileges are withdrawn for the time being too, Gemma.

Gemma   What privileges? Breathing? Using the bathroom?

Mrs Brogan   And Friday and Saturday night you can go out but you have to be back by nine o'clock.

Gemma   Oh can't we make it half past nine please?

Mrs Brogan   If you promise to make it half past nine *sharp* – okay? And the Saturday job is finished.

Gemma *opens her mouth – no sound.*

Mrs Brogan   Just till you get back on course.

Gemma   You just think I can't be trusted, but I did everything I could . . . .

Gemma *breaks down and cries. Exit* **Mr Brogan** *and* **Mrs Brogan**.

Gemma   Bastards, bastards, bastards!

Scene Three

Tar.

Music: The Clash, 'I'm Not Down'. **Tar** *hitches on the road to Bristol. Cars pass and eventually one stops for him.*

Scene Four

Mr Brogan, **Mrs Brogan**, **Gemma**, **Tar**.

Tar *is in a telephone box in Bristol.*

Mrs Brogan   The generosity is there Gemma, the love is there, the compromise. We don't like treating you like a child. All you have to do is show us you can follow a few simple rules and we can resume a happy family life. That's all we ask. (*To* **Mr Brogan**.) Come on darling, the court's booked for 6 p.m.

Mr Brogan   I'll get the car.

Exit parents.

Gemma (*to audience*)   My parents needed to be taught a lesson.

Phone rings, **Gemma** *snatches it up:* **Tar** *waiting to hear* **Gemma**'s *voice;* **Gemma**, *waiting to hear* **Tar**'s *voice.*

Pause.

Gemma   Hello?

Tar   Gemma! It's me . . . .

Gemma   Oh Tar I *miss* you, I *miss* you so much . . . . You all right?

Tar   Yeah, when are you coming Gemma?

Gemma   (*Pause.*)

Tar   Gemma?

Gemma   I'm coming, I'm coming . . . .

Tar   When?

Gemma   Soon as I can, Tar, soon as I can.

Tar   Maybe this weekend?

Gemma   Yeah, maybe.

Gemma *smiles very wide and can't stop smiling.* **Tar** *smiles and can't stop smiling. They can't speak. Each puts the receiver down.*

Scene Five

Tar.

By phone box, standing in a sleeping bag.

Tar (*to audience*)   I'd been feeling pretty down, being here in Bristol, sleeping rough, on my own. It was really depressing. But after the call, when I walked away from the phone box, I noticed the dandelions. They'd always been there, but I hadn't noticed them before. It was a solid mass of yellow, bright, golden yellow. Wild dandelions, not put there for me to look at, but there because they wanted to be there. All along the grubby street it was ablaze with yellow and everyone was walking up and down without even noticing them. It sounds stupid, but it was like the flowers had come out for Gemma. I love yellow. It's the colour of sunlight. I stood there staring at them, and I had an idea for a painting. A dandelion – just one huge bright yellow dandelion. It would be a big painting. I'm going to do it and give it to Gemma when she comes. And that big happy moment came swooping down, and I reached up a hand and caught hold of it and off I went. I picked a big bunch of dandelions. I felt great again. (*Beat.*) And *then* it hit me. I had nowhere to live.

Scene Six

Gemma.

At a table, on which are laid the relevant items.

Gemma (*to audience*)   Well, here it is – what you've all been waiting for, Gemma Brogan's practical handbook to running away from home. A step-by-step guide:

One. You will need: Clothes – woolly vest, plenty of keep-warm stuff. Plenty of underwear and other personal items. A waterproof coat. A personal stereo. A sleeping bag. A pencil and paper. Money. Your father's bank card and PIN number.

Two. Your wits. You'll need 'em.

Three. Think about it. What are your mum and dad going to do? Try to get you back of course. It'll be police. It'll be, oh, my God, my little girl has been abducted. It'll be, maybe some dreadful pervert is at her right now. Maybe she's lying murdered in a bin liner in the town rubbish tip THIS VERY SECOND! It never occurs to them that little Lucinda got so fed up with Mumsy and Dadsy that she actually left of her own accord. So . . . if you don't want every copper in the land on your tail and pictures of you shining out of all the national newspapers, you tell your mum and dad *exactly* what you're doing.

Four. This is where the pencil and paper comes in. You write them a note explaining that you're going away. Wish them luck, tell them no hard feelings and that you hope they will understand.

Five. Book your coach ticket using your father's Visa card.

Six. Go to the cash machine – take the money – and run.

Thank you very much.

Scene Seven

Richard, **Tar**, **Vonny**, **Jerry**.

It is dark, only street light. Hide-and-seek, hushed atmosphere.
Richard, **Vonny** *and* **Jerry** *are outside a terraced house.* **Tar**
joins them and crouches.

Richard (*to audience*)   Of course, property is a rather
strange concept for me. Especially if a fine house stands
empty and there's people sleeping on the streets. I know a
very nice nineteenth-century terraced house at the
Montpellier end of St Paul's. Come on up. (*To* **Tar**.) Here
we are.

Tar   Oh wow!

Richard   Always delighted to meet a new candidate for
the squatting movement.

Tar   Thanks, thanks . . . .

Richard   You'll be delighted to hear that we're going to
open a new squat tonight, right here in virgin territory.

Richard   I'm Richard and this is Vonny. (**Vonny** *appears
from hiding.*)

Vonny   Watcha.

Richard   This is Jerry. (**Jerry** *appears.*)

Jerry   All right?

Richard   We're anarchists. And you?

Tar   I'm Tar, just Tar.

Richard   Shush – get down.

Music, The Stranglers, 'Waltzin' Black', starts.

Richard *gets the window up and the boards off. They climb inside. It is pitch black. They talk in whispers.* **Richard** *hands out torches.*

Richard   Don't let anyone see the light from the street.

The three go to separate tasks – checking the electric and the gas, making sure the windows are sealed, seeing if they can get the back door open – it is an efficient operation, **Tar** *is amazed.*

(*to* **Tar**.) It's best to lie low for a couple of days until we're established. The longer we're here before they find out the better the chances of staying.

The three stick bottles with candles in them in different places, move boxes and suitcases around the space, roll out an old carpet.

(*to* **Tar**.) The idea is to get established as quickly as possible. It's a lot more difficult to eject us if we have a house full of stuff already.

They get the gas cooker going. **Jerry** *gets the lights on and all really see the place for the first time. They marvel at the house they have found.*

Tar   Wow! (*Pause.*) I think what you're doing is fantastic.

Richard *puts his music on a cassette player. They sit in a circle. It is now their home.* **Jerry** *passes round a joint.*

Vonny   So, when were you sixteen Tar?

Tar   I'm not sixteen. I'm only fourteen.

Richard   Oh dear. (*Pause.*) He should be locked up.

Tar   Who?

Richard   Your father of course, look what he's done to you.

Jerry   That means he can't sign on.

Tar   I've been begging, I want to find a job.

Richard   You'll just have to be a parasite off us for a couple of years.

Vonny   One more won't make any difference.

Richard   I'll bring home bits of work from the bicycle shop.

Jerry   Perhaps I can teach Tar some shoplifting techniques.

Richard   Oh, I don't think that would be a good idea, Jerry. If he gets caught he'll either get sent home or put into care, and we don't want that, do we?

Tar   My girlfriend wants to be with me too.

Vonny   How old is she?

Tar   Same as me.

Vonny   Fourteen?

Tar   Yeah, she doesn't look it though, she looks at least sixteen . . . .

Jerry   Why's she leaving her mum and dad, Tar? They beating her up as well?

Tar   No but they really drive Gemma mad, I mean . . . .

Jerry   The point is Tar, you're asking a lot of her, aren't you? She's got to give up her education, her parents, everything for you . . . .

Tar   It's not like that.

Jerry   I had arguments with my parents, too, but I didn't have to leave home.

Vonny   Do you want her to come very much?

Tar   I love her. (**Jerry** *laughs*.)

Jerry   He loves her!

Richard   We'll have a look at her, you're one of us now.

Vonny   He's only fourteen, Richard.

Richard   You can fall in love at any time. I was always falling in love at fourteen.

Vonny   Fourteen. Richard. She's only fourteen. She's not coming here. (*She looks hard at* **Jerry**.)

Jerry   Yeah right.

Tar (*pause*)   Can't she come then? Richard?

Richard   I'm sorry Tar. Tea?

Tar*'s head drops.*

Scene Eight

Gemma, **Mrs Brogan**, **Mr Brogan**.

Gemma (*to audience*)   This is how I did it.
I hid my bag in a garden a few houses down on Friday night, so I wouldn't be seen walking out with it. Next morning, shower, breakfast . . . .

Mr Brogan (*off*)   Where are you going this weekend?

Gemma   Down town, maybe.

Mrs Brogan (*off*)   I expect that boyfriend of yours is dead by now . . . sniffing glue or taking drugs . . . .

Mrs Brogan (*off*)   Stay out of trouble, Gemma.

Gemma   Bye Mum, bye Dad.

Mum/Dad (*off*)   Bye.

Gemma (*to audience*)   On the way to the station I dropped by the bank and got a hundred quid out. It was no sweat. In the town centre I posted the letter to my parents. Then I stepped on the coach. And the coach drove off. And it was as simple as that.

Gemma *sits on the coach and puts on earphones. She presses 'play' on Walkman. The Buzzcocks, 'Ever Fallen In Love With Someone' plays.* **Gemma** *looks out of the window and draws a heart on the glass.*

Scene Nine

Tar, **Jerry**, **Richard**, **Tar's mum** (*on phone*).

Tar *in a call box with pound coins.* **Jerry** *and* **Richard** *stand outside. He dials and waits. We hear* **Tar's mum** *as through a telephone.*

Tar   Hello.

Tar's mum (*back to audience, spotlight*)   David . . . .

Tar   Mum, it's me. I'm eating; I've got somewhere to live. The people are really fantastic. I'm eating. I'm looking after myself; really, I'm all right.

Pause.

Mum?

Sound of **Tar's mum** *sucking on cigarette.*

Tar   I'm sorry I went away. I didn't mean to . . . . I didn't want to, I mean. And . . . are you all right, Mum? Mum, say something won't you?

Tar's mum   I can't say much, David. He's upstairs listening. He's started to beat me. I've never been so scared. Every night he gets so drunk and I never know what he'll do next. It's so lonely. I can't get the housework done, darling. I try but you know what he's like . . . so fussy, so angry when things aren't right. It's not his fault; I've been a bad wife and a bad mother. You shouldn't have left me, David, you know that don't you?

Tar   Yes.

Tar's mum   You know how much I've relied on you . . . and I've been trying so hard . . . oh, darling, how could you . . . .

Tar   Listen, Mum . . . . Mum, just stop crying please and we'll talk about it. Is it bad, Mum? Is he hitting you a lot?

Tar's mum   Please come home David, please . . . . He's been saying that I drove you away . . .(*She is weeping and weeping.*)

Tar   All right, Mum, please stop . . . look, I'll come home, I'll come home. It's not forever. I'll come home. I'll come home. All right?

Tar's mum   When?

Tar   Soon as I can, Mum, there's just a couple of things I have to do first.

Tar's mum (*calm*)   You could leave now. Walk out of the phone box, get a coach.

Tar   I haven't got any money.

Tar's mum   Hitchhike.

Tar   I'll come as soon as I can.

Tar's mum   And you haven't got any money? But I thought you said you were all right . . . where are you, David . . . where are you living?

Tar   Mum, I can't exactly say now.

Tar's mum   Don't you trust me, David? Don't you trust me darling?

Tar *puts the phone down on his mum then turns and faces* **Richard** *and* **Jerry**.

Scene Ten

Gemma, Tar.

The Buzzcocks, 'Ever Fallen in Love With Someone' plays under scene.

Gemma (*to audience*)   The coach trip took hours. I was sitting there wetting my knickers all the way. Every time a police car came by I thought they were going to pull us over and arrest me and take me home. Then, at last we got to Bristol.

Gemma *on coach arriving in Bristol;* **Tar** *walking. Coach into bay and* **Tar** *looking for* **Gemma**. **Gemma** *in coach making sure* **Tar** *cannot see her.* **Gemma** *gets down off coach.*

Gemma   Tar! Tar!

Gemma *runs and leaps into the arms of* **Tar**. **Tar** *is overwhelmed.*

Gemma   Oh it's so good to see you . . . . Oh, I've MISSED you, I've MISSED you so much.

Gemma *and* **Tar** *walk around central Bristol. They go to the docks and enjoy the space and light.*
Traffic noises and The Buzzcocks under the following recorded voiceover:

Gemma   I made him walk me round a bit. We went through the town centre to the docks . . . and I just fell in love with the place. It wasn't big and busy like you think a city's gonna be. No one was desperate about anything. There were weeds growing out of the walls and people weren't rushing. I cooled down and I started feeling really mellow. I mean, I was still high, but it was okay to be high. No one was bothered about stopping me; it didn't feel like I was going out of control. I remember thinking, I'm gonna like it here. (*To* **Tar**.) We're free Tar, we're free, you, me, free, free, free . . .

She dances in the street.

Tar   They've cooked us a meal, they're really nice people.

Gemma *pulls* **Tar** *to her and makes* **Tar** *kiss her for a long time.*

Gemma   Wow . . . .

Tar   Yeah, wow . . . .

Gemma   I want you Tar, I want you now!

Tar   There's a lot of people . . . .

Gemma   That's okay Tar, 'cos there's always later
on . . . .

Tar (*smiles*)   Yeah that's right, we got all night . . . .

Gemma   Oh, Tar all night, and all day and all week and,
what's more – I've got a lovely present for you Tar!

Tar *and* **Gemma** *snog in the middle of the street again.*

Scene Eleven

Tar, **Gemma**, **Vonny**, **Richard**, **Jerry**, **Mr Brogan**.

They arrive at the squat. **Richard**, **Vonny** *and* **Jerry** *are around
the oven together.* **Tar** *introduces* **Gemma** *to* **Vonny**, **Vonny**
gives **Gemma** *a motherly kiss and a protective hug.* **Tar** *introduces*
Gemma *to* **Jerry***; big smiles no physical contact.* **Tar** *introduces*
Gemma *to* **Richard***;* **Richard** *looks everywhere but at*
Gemma *and smiles madly.* **Gemma** *giggles and looks at* **Tar**.

Tar   This is Gemma.

Gemma   Gemma Brogan, hiya.

Tar   This is Vonny.

Vonny   Hi.

Tar   That's Jerry. That's Richard.

Richard   Hi, good to meet you.

Gemma Hi, Richard. (*Whispers in* **Tar**'s *ear.*) Is it the fashion to be *nice* here?

Tar Gemma . . . .

Gemma Just joking.

Vonny *is at the oven preparing the meal.*

Vonny It's very dry I'm afraid – where've you been, Tar?

Gemma/Tar (*in unison*) We've been sightseeing and –

Vonny Richard made a lentil bake –

Richard Vonny it's OK, it's –

Tar Sorry, Rich, sorry.

Richard Oh that's all right. (*Mad smiling.*)

Pause.

Vonny How long are you staying with us Gemma?

All look at **Gemma**, *casually, in pause.*

Gemma I don't know, I just don't know, it depends how you treat me!

Everyone smiles at everyone else, awkwardly.

An instant adjustment. They are squashed in a pub together. Some two to three hours later; ambience of pub, Ian Dury, 'Hit Me With Your Rhythm Stick' plays, they shout to each other. The conversation has been going on for some time.

Richard (*in answer to* **Jerry**) My parents used to let me misbehave all I wanted (*Mad grin.*), I made plenty of use of the opportunity. (*Laughter – except* **Tar**.)

Jerry Don't you start worrying about your mum again, Tar, you're staying put.

Vonny Listen to him, Tar.

Gemma (*to brighten the moment*) Mine'll be grinding their teeth, raging round the house and phoning all my friends, because I am a whole hour late. (*To the bar.*) Oh, a Pernod and Black for me.

Vonny   Don't you think you ought to ring your folks up and tell them you're all right?

Gemma   What for?

Vonny   But they must be feeling awful. At least you could let them know you're all right.

Gemma   And tell them what? When to expect me back? And where to send the woolly vests.

Vonny   No, like I said – just let them know you're okay.

Richard   I think that would be a good idea.

Gemma *looks to* **Tar** *for help;* **Tar** *nods in agreement to* **Vonny**'s *suggestion.* **Vonny** *finds a coin and holds out hand:* **Jerry** *and* **Richard** *both put in one pound too.* **Gemma** *at payphone.* **Mr Brogan** *at home on phone.*

Gemma (*at coin slot of phone, in anger*)   Pig! Pig! Pig!

Mr Brogan   Gemma . . . where have you been? Where are you now?

Gemma   I'm all right, I'm just –

Mr Brogan   We've been worried sick –

Gemma   It's only half past ten –

Mr Brogan   It's eleven o'clock and you should have been in an hour and a half ago. I thought we were past this, I thought things were getting better. Your mother . . . .

Gemma   Look, I'm ringing up to let you know I won't be back tonight . . . .

Mr Brogan   You . . . you'd better be back. Picked up with some of those seafront friends again, have you . . . ? It isn't good enough, Gemma.

Gemma *holds the phone away from her ear, hand over speaker, looks to ceiling.*

Gemma   Please don't do this to me . . . .

They are all watching **Gemma**. *She pretends to have a normal conversation.*

Gemma   Oh, we're having a great time, thanks. Yes, okay, I'll be careful. Yeah, thanks, Dad. I'll ring you tomorrow . . . Yeah, big kiss to Mum . . . .

Mr Brogan   Why are you speaking to me like that, are you being sarcastic? Gemma, what's going on? Look, let's overlook this slip. You get back here WITHIN THE HOUR and we can discuss –

Gemma   No, I've already eaten, we had baked potatoes. I'll give you a ring again, tomorrow probably. Okay, see you, Dad, thanks, bye . . . .

Mr Brogan   Gemma! (**Gemma** *puts the phone down on her dad.*)

Vonny   Are you okay? Gemma? Is everything okay at home?

Gemma   Look, I've done it. Is that enough for you?

Vonny *thinks about it and nods. Exit* **Gemma**, *past* **Vonny**.

Scene Twelve

Tar, **Gemma**.

Tar *and* **Gemma** *in bedroom. Candlelight.* **Gemma** *puts bedroll down next to the mattress.*

Tar   Do you want to go to sleep?

Neither moves. Both awkward.

Gemma   Okay. Tar, let's light candles.

Tar (*with enthusiasm*) Yeah!

They arrange candles and bedding and make the room cosy.

Tar (*suddenly*) I'll be back in a minute.

Gemma *pauses alone, and undresses fast. In the bag she takes off her knickers and T-shirt and then wraps the sleeping bag right up to her nose.* **Tar** *comes in wearing his pants and socks.*

Tar Do you want a cuddle?

Gemma All right, then.

Tar *gets into the sleeping bag with* **Gemma**.

Tar (*startled*) You've got nothing on.

Gemma That's my present, Tar.

Tar Oh!

They cuddle and get intimate.

Gemma Have you got anything?

Tar Oh shit!

She sits up in bed.

Gemma Do I have to do everything?

Tar I'm sorry, I'm just so stupid. Hang on . . . .

Tar *leaves the room.*

She shouts after him but he's already shut the door behind him.

Gemma Oh no, Tar, no, Tar, Tar . . . . I don't want to use boring old borrowed anarchist condoms! This is my first time . . . .

Heated conversation from the landing.

Tar Has anyone got a condom?

Jerry You can't, you're too young, Tar.

Vonny No.

Richard   I might have one somewhere.

Vonny   He's too young Richard.

Richard   It's better to be safe than sorry, we don't want an unwanted pregnancy, do we?

Jerry   Yeah, right.

Vonny   *Richard!*

Tar   Thanks Rich.

Jerry   Good luck, Tar.

Tar *re-enters the room.*

Tar   Sorry.

Gemma   What happened?

Tar   They were a bit reluctant to lend them.

Gemma   Why?

Tar   Well, you're only fourteen, see, and they were just worried . . . .

Gemma   I get the picture.

Pause. She turns away.

Tar   Don't you want to anymore?

Gemma   Oh never mind.

Tar *leans over.*

Tar   I love you.

Gemma   Ssssh . . . . Don't say that.

Tar   Dandelion.

Gemma   What's that supposed to mean?

Tar *smiles and shrugs and* **Gemma** *smiles back.*

Gemma   Ladybird.

Tar Why ladybird?

Gemma Because they're nice, and everyone likes them, and they're pretty and red . . . .

They begin to kiss.

Gemma And they like dandelions a lot.

Gemma *touches his nose with the tip of her finger.* **Tar** *smiles and nods.*

Tar Dandelion.

Gemma Ladybird.

Tar Dandelion.

Gemma Ladybird.

Tar *gets into the double bag and they blow the candle out.*

Scene Thirteen

Richard, **Vonny**, **Jerry**, **Gemma**, **Tar**.

Richard *appears in 'Glue You' T-shirt, pair of bright-green Doc Marten's with daisies on the toes, tight calf-length leggings; several tubes of Locktite in pockets.* **Vonny** *in yellow and black striped leotard and woolly tights.* **Jerry** *in black, and black mascara and eyeshadow.* **Gemma** *in party dress and big make-up.* **Tar** *adds a long scarf and hat. Music: The Stranglers, 'Waltzin' Black'.*

Richard (*to audience*) This is a stick-up. We're out to glue the banks. This is the way a stick-up ought to be. Not Bonnie and Clyde. Not gangsters and the IRA and BANG BANG BANG you're dead. More like Robin Hood. I mean the Disney version.

They all follow **Richard** *to a door. He removes a sign from his bag and reads it to them:*

'Bristol anarchists say, "Go back to bed".' My tools are Superglue and subversion. No one gets hurt, everyone has a good time, including my victims. They get the day off work.

All follow him as if walking down the street. They listen to their leader.

When you walk down a high street in Bristol, you have so much going on around you. Butcher's shops, for example. I'm a vegan myself. It's an issue. Streetlights blazing away, burning up the fossil fuels. Banks and insurance companies investing in death and disease. Chemists selling cosmetics that have been dripped in monkey's eyes. Plenty of opportunity for Vonny to spread a bit of political awareness. (*Pause.*) And overhead the stars. It was a lovely night. Come on let's DO IT!

Scenes of action, **Jerry** *and* **Gemma** *smoking and fooling around. They stick up other signs: 'The Bristol anarchist collective invites you to go back to bed. Have a good day!' and 'No work today . . . don't tell me you're disappointed?'*

Vonny   Jerry's smoking.

Richard   Oh. When is Jerry not smoking?

Vonny   Yes but he's giving some to Gemma.

Richard   Oh dear.

Vonny   What shall we do?

Richard   Play it by ear.

Jerry   Hey, Richard. This is the Co-operative Bank . . . do we still glue it up?

Richard   They're still a bank.

Jerry   Yeah, but they're the Co-operative Bank.

Richard   They're still a bank, Jerry.

Jerry   What about South Africa?

Richard   Glue it!

Gemma *giggles loudly, and trips and giggles loudly again.*

Vonny   She's only fourteen. You can imagine the mess the police or the press would make of it.

Richard   Corrupting the youth of the nation you mean.

Vonny   Exactly.

Richard   But we are. (*He kisses* **Vonny**.)

Freeze action.

Richard (*to audience*)   You may think I am being a bit of a prat. I am. I'm fishing for hearts and souls. The bank manager's heart. The bank clerk's. For Tar's, for Gemma's, for Vonny's, for Jerry's. And yes, for yours too. Go on, be a devil. Do your bit. Stay in bed today.

Gemma *collapses, drunk and stoned, she pukes.*

Lovely life, isn't it?

He puts her over his shoulder and carries her off.

Scene Fourteen

Vonny, **Gemma**, **Tar**.

Vonny (*to audience*)   You don't get any space when Gemma's around, she fills it all up. She's a spoilt brat, she doesn't have problems, not real ones, not like Tar has. When you're fourteen years old you belong to someone – your parents! She ought to be at school, at home and tucked up in bed.

Exit **Vonny**. **Gemma** *and* **Tar** *are painting a wall of the squat.* **Gemma** *pauses to speak to the audience:*

Gemma   We were having a WILD TIME. Glueing the banks. Sharing the washing up, eating baked potatoes and beans for dinner every day. WOW . . . Nah . . . it was all right, really. But, you know, where's the wild parties, where's the street life, where's the CITY? But then, Tar was having such a great time. I think he was in heaven. And we were getting on really well. I've got painty finger marks all over.

They fool around with paint and grope. **Gemma** *starts again.* **Tar** *pauses to speak to the audience:*

Tar   We can stay up as late as we like and we can get up when we want. We can be together all day and all night. Since we've got no money and they're feeding us, we're doing the house up. Richard found the paint somewhere, liberated it he said.

They fool around more and land up on top of each other. They are really about to make love.

Vonny (*from off*)   TAR! Come and help with the shopping.

Gemma *stands back ostentatiously to allow* **Tar** *to go to* **Vonny**.

Gemma   Mummy calls . . . .

Tar *torn between* **Vonny** *and* **Gemma**. **Tar** *exits.*

Gemma (*to audience*)   Actually, Richard and Vonny make a perfectly reasonable set of parents. As parents they're perfect. The only trouble is I haven't run away from home to find a new set. It's boring. They're always worrying about how legal we are. I want to meet some people my own age. Time to change. Time to spend. (*Takes out money and kisses it.*) Thanks Dad.

Scene Fifteen

Gemma.

Music / movement sequence – **Gemma** *becomes a punk. Scene choreographed to same length as The Only Ones, 'Another Girl, Another Planet'. She strips to pants and bra and builds up a whole new look. The rest of the cast become market traders who help her don the following: studs in ears, nose and hair, short black skirt, huge black*

*boots, granddad T-shirt with black laces, black tights, black lipstick
and eyeliner. She transforms her identity before our eyes.* **Gemma**
looks in mirror:

Gemma   Mmmm! I can't ever go home now.

Scene Sixteen

Tar, **Gemma**.

Tar *sits at a café table. Café music.* **Gemma** *sits at table next to
him. She smokes.* **Tar** *stares past* **Gemma**. **Gemma** *stares at
him hard, as if she fancies him.* **Tar** *gets nervous.* **Gemma** *gives
him a little wink.* **Tar** *blushes.* **Tar** *then gives* **Gemma** *a sickly
little smile.* **Tar** *catches her eye again.* **Gemma** *gets up to sit next to
him.*

Tar   GEMMA!?

Gemma   Who do you think? Come on.

Tar *is gobsmacked.*

Gemma   Well come on then.

Tar   I haven't paid for my tea.

Gemma   Fuck it!

They get up and walk together. **Tar** *kisses* **Gemma** *his hands all
over her.*

Gemma   This is practically being unfaithful. No, you'll
smudge my lipstick. Is this the place?

Gemma *opens doors to a punk club playing incredibly loud music.
Everyone pogoes to 'Skin Up for Jesus'.* **Gemma** *speaks loudly
through a hand mike above the din.*

We'd stumbled on this real punk den more or less by
accident. You could tell the girls who were the real punks.
They looked like absolute slags. They didn't care about
anything. I felt completely over-dressed.

Gemma *rips her fishnets and throws her jacket off.*

And the band. They were just so obscene and rude and wonderful. The music was like being beaten up, only it didn't hurt, you know what I mean.

Gemma *and* **Tar** *pogo.*

I just screamed with pleasure.

Gemma *and* **Tar** *pogo together.* **Tar** *slowly vanishes, only* **Gemma** *now.*

I couldn't see Tar anymore but that didn't matter. I pushed my way right up into the crush at the front of the stage and pogoed up and down and started spitting at the singer with all the others. It was great but it was so hot and hard up there you couldn't stay for long.

The music ends. The crowd exit, shouting. **Gemma** *stands with one of the guys who was pogoing. She crosses to* **Tar**.

Gemma   Someone's asked me back to their place. Here, have you got your bus fare? (*Pause.* **Tar** *is silent.*) You're not my bloody mother either.

Gemma *rejoins bloke.* **Gemma** *exits.* **Tar** *stays motionless, hurt so much he can't move. Pause.* **Gemma** *runs back in alone and grabs him.*

Gemma   You should have seen your face!

Scene Seventeen

Vonny, **Gemma**, **Tar**, **Richard**, **Jerry**.

Vonny (*to audience*)   I was furious with her when she came back from that bop, dressed in leather and all the rest. We'd been feeding her, paying her bills, we'd even been supplying her with fags.

Gemma   It's my party clothes.

Vonny   This isn't a party, and I'm not your mother.

Gemma *pulls a face at* **Vonny**.

Vonny (*to audience*)   My feeling was, it was important to get her back home before she really took off. You could see that she was going to go over the top. Just walking down the street, you could see her peering over heads at anyone she thought might be interesting, fighting her way to a shop that looked 'her sort of place'. Jerry, of course, was totally useless. He liked having a young girl around to get stoned with, that was about as far as it went. Poor old Tar didn't stand a chance in hell to find out what sort of person he was, of course, and *he* was the one who really needed to. Tar was important – he was in trouble. We had it out with her the night before the party. I more or less had to do it on my own.

Vonny *is talking to* **Gemma**. **Jerry** *and* **Richard** *are silent.*

Vonny   You've had your fun Gemma – and you're welcome to stay for the party. But then Richard, Jerry and I feel that you should go back home to Minely-on-Sea.

Gemma   But why?

Vonny   Because it isn't fair on us . . . you're only fourteen and it's not as if you're being kicked around like Tar would be if he went back.

Gemma   You don't know what my parents are like –

Vonny   Okay they're making life unnecessarily hard.

Gemma   Unnecessarily hard? I can't do anything . . . .

Vonny   Running away from your problems isn't going to solve them Gemma. It's time to go home.

Gemma   Don't tell me what to do, you ridiculous creepy woman.

Vonny   Now look Gemma, we've fed you, we've hidden you, we've even broken the law for you.

Gemma   Oh nob off, Vonny.

Vonny   Gemma if you like I'll phone your parents – you can trust me not to say . . . .

Gemma   I wouldn't trust you with a roll of toilet paper.

Vonny (*to audience*)   Well, what more could we do?

Shift.

Tar   I don't want you to go, you know I don't want you to go.

Gemma   Then what are you on about?

Tar   But they're right.

Shift.

Richard   I've found a few people their age to ask to the party.

Vonny   Oh great, who?

Richard   Oh you know . . . that bunch on City Road.

Vonny   The ones you introduced me to?

Richard   That's right

Vonny   Richard!

Richard   What?

Pause.

Vonny   Have you looked into their eyes?

Richard   Why?

Vonny (*to audience*)   Of course, Richard never looked anyone in the face.

Scene Eighteen

Richard, **Tar**, **Gemma**, **Vonny**, **Lily**, **Rob**.

Party music cuts in loud. Central focus is on how much **Gemma** *consumes. She is spotlit throughout.* **Vonny** *and* **Richard** *are at the oven, cooking.* **Tar** *crosses from side to side with cans and bottles.* **Richard** *removes a tray from the oven.*

Richard   Hash cakes!

Everyone takes one. **Richard** *and* **Tar** *exit. During the activity* **Gemma** *has another, then smokes a joint. Enter* **Tar** *and* **Richard**, *both excited.*

Tar   We're going to open a new squat.

Gemma   What for? We've got one!

Tar   No, you don't understand, it's just to free up as many properties as we can.

Gemma   We're having a party! Why make all this if you're not going to stay.

Tar *grins, speechless, caught between his love for* **Richard** *and his love for her.*

Gemma   You look really weird, Tar, are you all right, are you all right?

Tar   Yeah.

Tar *dashes off following* **Richard** *and looking at* **Gemma**.

Gemma (*to audience*)   This is unreal. This is a squat, and they're running away from my last night on earth.

Gemma *picks up a bottle of vodka and swigs. She relights her joint and inhales deeply, then she swigs more vodka.*

Tar   Is anything wrong? What's the problem Gemma?

Gemma   Oh just shut up, why can't you leave me alone?

Sound becomes very loud and surreal. Light goes to orange as **Gemma** *stands centre stage looking ill. She drops a lit joint into a bottle of wine – she can't take anymore. Music creates a nauseous climax so that we see these moments from* **Gemma**'s *point of view.* **Gemma**'s *voiceover is heard above everything:*

Wow – This is something – I don't like it that much – But it's something – I'm stoned – I'm stoned out of my fucking head.

Lights change again. Music, The Stranglers, 'Golden Brown'. Enter **Lily**, *dancing. She is moving to the music, dancing, swaying her head, just really going with the music. She can't stand still, she is smiling all the time, not at anyone, just to herself. She dances over to* **Rob** *and kisses him and rubs up to him. She is different to everyone.* **Gemma** *almost bursts out laughing because of what* **Lily** *is wearing.* **Lily** *is wearing a black net string vest. Everyone is watching her.*

Gemma (*to audience*)   Did you ever see someone and think straight away, I want to be that person? I want to look like her and think like her and have the same effect as she does . . . you know? This girl – nothing mattered to her. All the rules, all the things you do and don't do, the manners, everything – she had none of that. She didn't have to say please or thank you. She didn't have to be offered anything; it was already hers. She was more herself than anyone else ever was and as soon as I clapped eyes on her I knew I wanted to be myself just as much as she was herself.

Lily *is there, dancing in front of* **Gemma**, *moving her head to the music in front of her.*

Lily   Hi, what's your party like?

Gemma   Great.

Gemma *starts giggling just as she gets her drink to her mouth and splutters it all over herself.*

Lily   Can I have some of that?

Gemma   Sure.

Gemma *gets herself another drink.*

Lily Hey, you don't need that stuff you know.

Gemma I know, I know, I don't know what I'm doing.

Lily You're doing okay, you know that.

Gemma I know, I know . . . .

Lily Hey, Hey. (**Gemma** *starts crying.*)

Lily *puts her arms around* **Gemma** *and hugs her. She holds her close.* **Gemma** *hugs her straight back and gets tearful.*

Yeah, isn't that great? Isn't that great? Music's the only drug . . . yeah . . . . Come on let's see what's going on . . . .

Lily *breaks away and moves to the door, still dancing.* **Gemma** *follows her through.* **Lily** *plucks a joint from* **Vonny**'s *fingers and stands next to* **Gemma**. **Gemma** *has a couple of puffs.* **Lily** *takes it off her.*

You don't need that either. (*Points.*) That's my man there, Rob. He's on the right side, you know.

Tar *enters.*

Tar Oh there you are. We went out to have a look at the new squat but you were asleep. Are you all right?

Gemma This is Lily.

Tar (*doesn't know where to look*) Yeah, hi, hello. Yeah, really nice to meet you.

Lily Those are a really nice pair of boots.

Tar Are they?

Lily Yeah, I love 'em.

Tar Thanks.

Tar *stands there looking awkward and unhappy while* **Lily** *closes her eyes and dances with her head.*

Gemma He's the one I ran away with.

Lily Oh right . . . . Yeah that's great everyone should run away, you did the right thing, I did when I was twelve. You did the right thing for Gemma too.

Gemma Yeah if it wasn't for Tar, I'd still be at home going mad. Tar had a really bad time at home; he got knocked around by his dad.

Rob Yeah, right . . . leave the bastard.

Lily (*very close to* **Tar**) Well done, man, you broke the door down . . . brilliant, brilliant, yeah!

Rob (*suddenly, powerfully*) Brilliant. I love you, man, I love you.

Tar *is intimidated.*

Gemma It's all right Tar, it's all right. (*Happily.*) Everyone was staring at *us*.

Lily Sod this, let's go. Come on . . . . This place is dead.

Tar But all our things are here.

Lily They'll be here tomorrow or you can get some new things . . . .

Rob That's right, you put your order in.

Lily Come on, Gemma.

Everyone heads for the door. **Vonny** *glares at* **Gemma**.

Gemma Yeah!

Scene Nineteen

Lily, **Gemma**, **Tar**, **Rob**.

The street – **Men** *shout at* **Lily** *and* **Gemma**. **Rob** *and* **Tar** *ignore it.*

Man SLAGS! PUNK SLAGS!

Lily (*cheerfully*)   Fuck off beer monsters!

Gemma   Yeah, fuck off!

Rob *looks cool about it, the girls can handle it.* **Tar** *looks shaken and unsure.* **Gemma** *walks very excitedly with* **Lily**, *they are grabbing hold of each other, giggling, talking, and laughing. They are ahead,* **Lily** *is shooting looks at* **Tar**, **Tar** *knows he is being talked about.*

Tar   Lily's your girlfriend yeah . . . ? She's . . . .

Rob   Yeah, no one's found the right word for Lils yet. But what about Gemma? You'd think they'd been mates for about a thousand years.

Tar   Yeah . . . .

Rob   They're an amazing pair of girls right?

Tar   Yeah . . . .

Rob *puts his arm around* **Tar** *and* **Tar** *cheers up a bit.*

Gemma *and* **Lily** *come over to* **Tar**. **Gemma** *is just behind* **Lily**, *something is afoot.*

Lily   You did it.

Tar   Did I? What?

Lily   They were trying to turn you into an animal but you broke out, you got away!

Tar   Yeah?

Lily   You're the bloody Titanium Man! Yeah . . . . Tar, you're the Titanium Man!

Lily *grabs his arm and sticks it up in the air.* **Tar** *tries to pull it down but she pushes it back up and dances around him.*

Rob   Yeah that's right man, you got away, you did it!

Rob *is grinning and nodding.*

Gemma   She means it, Tar, you did the most amazing thing. You did it, you did it . . . .

Lily   I don't know how you can be so strong, you really did it, man. And here you are and the rest of your life is gonna be so GREAT! And you're so sexy and I love you, man, I love, mmmm, yeah, I don't know how anyone can resist you you're so GREAT! You did it!

Lily *grabs hold of* **Tar** *and pulls his head down and starts kissing him and pushing into him like he is a pop star.* **Rob** *is cheering and* **Gemma** *is cheering too.*

Mmm, mmm, you're so SEXY, you're so STRONG, you're the Titanium Man.

Tar *kisses* **Lily**'s *back and rubs his hand all over her, finally letting go of his uncertainty and shyness.*

Tar   I DID it! I did it . . . I got away . . . I did it . . . . Yeahhhhhhh!

Scene Twenty

Rob, **Lily**, **Gemma**, **Tar**.

Tar *asleep on the sofa at* **Rob** *and* **Lil**'s *squat.* **Gemma** *and* **Lily** *in deep communication.*

Rob (*to audience*)   It was the weekend, not that I care what day it is. A day's a day. We get out of bed maybe one o'clock. I had a bit of business later on, but till then it was okay sitting around, listening to music, people watching. That's half my life.
We'd stayed up after Tar had fallen asleep, and Gems was telling us all about it – him and her. How he loved her but she didn't love him, but she didn't want to hurt him because she liked him so much, all that stuff.
Basically, Gems was feeling a bit tied down. I could see what she meant. Tar'd had a hard time. He wanted to lie low for a bit. But Gems – she wanted to take the place by storm.

Tar *wakes up and goes off to bed, still high from* **Lily**. **Gemma** *kisses him goodnight but stays put in the room.*

Lily   Gems, why don't you come and live here with us?

Rob   Yeah why not?

Gemma   Do you mean that? Do you really mean that? I'd love to live here, I'd love to live with you.

Gemma *is ecstatic and lies on the sofa with* **Lily** *and* **Rob**.

Rob (*to audience*)   And it felt just right, you know. As soon as the idea was floated we all knew it was right. We got into this big hug on the sofa. 'Welcome home Gems', and I rolled a giant ten-skinner to celebrate. After, Lils and I did a chase when Gems had fallen asleep. We were doing too much really, but we'd been bingeing that weekend and it's important to come down slowly.

Gemma *is left asleep on the sofa.* **Rob** *and* **Lily** *exit to chase.*

Scene Twenty-one

Richard, **Vonny**, **Tar**.

Tar *is sitting with crayons and a board on his knees. He is drawing a dandelion, big and bright, but without much success.* **Vonny** *comes in.*

Richard   Hello, Tar.

Vonny   Hello, Tar. How are you?

Tar   Okay.

Vonny   Where's Gemma?

Tar   She's not coming back.

Vonny   They're scum.

Tar   They look a bit scummy, but they're not really like that.

Vonny   I wouldn't like to find one of them in my shoe in the morning.

Tar   I liked them.

Richard   Oh dear.

Vonny   It's Gemma that I really blame –

Richard   Maybe it's all for the best, Vonny . . . .

Vonny   That girl . . . .

Tar   She just wants to fly . . . .

Vonny *exits*.

Richard   Oh dear . . . .

Tar (*to* **Richard**)   So do I . . . .

Pause. Exit **Richard**.

Scene Twenty-two

Lily, **Tar**, **Gemma**, **Rob**.

Lily *brings* **Tar** *back to her place.* **Lily** *is carrying a tray of candles and a lit taper. She puts the tray of candles on the front of the stage.*

Lily   Come with me.

Tar   How's Gemma?

Lily   Oh, she's great, she's fantastic, you know our Gems (*She laughs.*), don't get all hung up on the romantic love stuff.

Lily *starts clutching at her heart and her throat and moaning.*

My life is at an end, I cannot go on without her, oh woe, oh woe . . . .

She ends up leaning backwards with her hand at her throat and her tongue hanging out. **Tar** *laughs.*

She's been missing you, we all have. And me.

Lily *kisses* **Tar** *on the lips. A real long kiss. She puts her arm in* **Tar***'s and pushes her body against his.*

We're home! You can open your eyes now.

Gemma *ambushes* **Tar**.

Gemma   I missed you, I really missed you, I was so AMAZED at how much I missed you.

They embrace.

Rob *and* **Lily** *shower* **Tar** *and* **Gemma** *with dandelions.*

Tar   For me?

Rob/Gemma/Lily   For you! For you!

Lily   Yeah, and now you've got three people to love instead of just one.

Gemma *claps her hands and whoops,* **Rob** *yells.*

Rob   Yeah, yeah!

Tar *starts crying, he looks at* **Gemma**. **Lily** *stands on tiptoes and licks all the tears off* **Tar***'s face.*

Lily   Hey Tar, hey, hey. I'm gonna live forever now.

Rob *is shaking something on to a bit of foil.* **Lily** *starts lighting candles.*

Candles are magic, I collect magic.

Rob *hands the foil to* **Lily**. *She lights a match and holds it underneath the foil. A thick curl of white smoke rises from the foil.* **Lily** *holds the foil near to her mouth and she sucks down the curl of white smoke and clamps her lips down.*

Glop!

She holds her breath for ages. Then she breathes out slowly, sensually.

Now I feel good. (*She smiles.*)

Tar   What is it?

Lily *waves her fingers in the air like it was spooky and magic.*

Lily   Heroin, yeah!

Tar   Is it? Is it really heroin? Is it?

Rob *starts doing another lot.* **Rob** *holds out the foil for* **Gemma***, she grins at* **Tar***, strikes a match and does the same as* **Lily***.*

Gems!?

Gemma   Glop!

Gemma *lets the smoke ooze out of her nostrils.*

Lily   Don't let it go, don't let it go . . . !

Gemma *chases the smoke she'd let out with her mouth.*

Rob   That's important smoke.

Rob *does one for* **Tar***,* **Tar** *shakes his head,* **Rob** *laughs and sucks it down himself.*

Lily   Hey! Hey, that's Tar's; what're you doing?

Rob *just smiles, opens his mouth and lets the smoke out. He gets out a little packet and shakes it at her.*

Rob   Plenty more where that came from.

Gemma   Go on, try it, it won't hurt. It doesn't do you any harm, it just makes you feel good.

Tar   I don't want to.

Lily   Aren't you gonna be a junkie with us? Are you a junkie, Tar?

Tar   No.

Lily   A little heroin isn't going to change you into one. You have to think like a junkie if you want to be a junkie.

Rob   Yeah, you don't need junk to help you . . . .

Gemma *sighs and leans back in her chair.*

Gemma   It's all right Tar, it's all right. You don't have to do it ever again if you don't want to. But try it once. Try everything once. All that stuff you hear about one little hit and you're a junkie for life is just stories, you know.

Lily   Stories to tell the kids, stories to keep you in your place.

Rob *does another one. He holds it out for* **Tar**.

Rob   Junk's the best. That's why the doctors keep it for themselves.

He gives **Tar** *a slow wink.*

Lily   Look, he's actually going to miss the chance to feel better than anyone else in the whole world.

Rob   More for us.

Rob *holds the lighter for* **Tar**, *lights it up, holds it under the foil.* **Tar** *watches and then he inhales the white smoke.*

Tar   Glop.

Tar *reacts violently, then becomes calm and very still.*

Lily   Breathe, Breathe.

Gemma   Better?

Tar   Yeah!

Gemma *comes and sits next to* **Tar** *and wriggles under his arm.*

Gemma   Tar, will you go out with me?

Tar   Yeah, I will.

Gemma   I nearly blew that didn't I?

Lily   You're gonna live here now, with us. Both of you. Yeah?

Tar   Yeah!

Lily (*to audience: magical, soft and persuasive*)   Sometimes I look out of the window and I see all of the straights crawling past,

going to work, coming back from work, going to learn how
to go to work, whatever. And I want to shout out, 'Hey!
Listen to me! It's not like that, it really isn't like that . . . .'
Only I never do it. It's useless. They must weigh about sixty
thousand tons. I'm so far away from people like that, they
can't even see me.

Listen. You can *be* anything you want to be. Be careful.
It's a spell. It's magic. You can be *anything*. You can *do*
anything.

Listen to the magic. You *are* anything. Whatever you
want. I've done everything. You think it, I've done it. All the
things you never dared, all the things you dream about, all
the things you were curious about and then forgot because
you knew you never would. I did 'em, I did 'em yesterday
while you were still in bed. What about you? When's it
gonna be *your* turn?

End of Act One.

Act Two

Scene One

Gemma, **Tar**, **Lily**.

Montage of several months of living, partying and enjoying junk, friends and freedom. Snaps are taken for the photo album. Music, New Order, 'Blue Monday'.

Gemma (*to audience*) You should come round to our place sometime. You'd love it, everyone does, it's a party. At night we light the fire. There's always something going on – dealing, music, people. There's Dev the dealer. (*Light on Dev.*) He doesn't go out much but he sometimes comes and sits by the fire and rolls joint after joint. Then there's Sal. (*Light on Sal.*) She used to be with Dev but they split up. I get on really well with Sal, she's right on my wavelength. We're almost as close as me and Lily – almost. Dev's okay, he's a bit boring; he does too much stuff, I reckon. He could be a casualty. Well you get casualties. Life's a dangerous business.

Tar *comes forward from party.*

Tar (*to audience*) When she took me back I was so happy. I was just so happy. And when I came back, she was in love with me as much as I was in love with her. We were all in love with one another. We were in love with ourselves. We still are.

Gemma *comes out from party.*

Gemma (*to audience*) I really love him. When I think how close I came to chucking him! It was a close thing. I must have been crazy. I guess I was so excited, I felt that everything had to be different after I met Lily and Rob. It was them who talked me out of it.

Lily You gotta look after him, he's yours, can't you see that?

Gemma   Yeah. He's mine. We got each other. I'm his.

Tar *comes out from party.*

Tar (*to audience*)   I still love her, but it's different now. I don't need her anymore, you know. If she chucked me now, I'd still be really upset, but I know that I'd get on with my life. Back then it felt like the end of the world.
When I moved here, I remember thinking, I'm in control now. It was the first time I felt I had my own life in my own hands. There I was, scrabbling and struggling to keep things together. These days, I just let go of them.

Snap immediately to **Gemma**.

Gemma (*to audience*)   Junk's the best. I mean the BEST. You've got to be special to use it. You could sit in a sewer all day and be so happy and feel so good. Look, drugs are fun. Sure they're powerful, that's why they're dangerous. So's *life*!

Tar *comes out from party.*

Tar (*to audience*)   I do worry about Gemma. I mean, I can take it or leave it but she never says no. Of course we never use needles, we've got more sense than that. It'll be all right. I just have to remember I got away from my mum and dad. If I can escape from that, I can escape from anything.

Party time, which breaks up during **Gemma**'s *speech.*

Gemma (*to audience*)   We're all skint, really skint. We'd been having a bit of a binge that week, too much really, but it's nice to do too much once in a while. After you've done a junk binge, you feel it. You feel horrible. Just horrible. I mean horrible.

Scene Two

Lily, **Gemma**, **Rob**, **Tar**, **Sal**.

Tar *and* **Gemma** *are sitting on the sofa. The TV is on and 'The Clangers' is playing. Enter* **Lily***, in string vest and coat, she throws paper money at the ceiling, it cascades over the floor.* **Rob** *enters with gear and cooks up.*

Lily   Free money, free money!

Lily *jives round the room.*

Gemma   How did you get it? How did you get it?

Lily *keeps jiving and does not answer.*

Gemma   Did you rob someone or not? Did you?

Lily *does not answer.*

Lily   Sixty quid, not bad for half an hour's work, eh Gems?

Gemma   Go on then, tell me, I've been going mad.

Lily   I turned over a punter.

Gemma (*to* **Tar**)   What's that mean? Did she mug someone? Or what? (*To* **Lily***.*) Tell me!

Lily   I've been a little prossie for half an hour, that's all.

Gemma (*gob smacked*)   What did you do? Who with for Christ's sake? Where did you go? Have you done it before? Did you enjoy it?

Lily (*snaps*)   It's a job Gems, nobody likes working.

Gemma   All right. So how do you do it?

Rob *continues to cook up.*

Lily   You stand on the street corner.

Rob   I wait a little bit down the road.

Lily The punter comes along in his car, winds down his window, he has a little chat – Rob makes himself seen.

Rob So the punter knows she ain't alone.

Lily He's seen the goods so we decide on the service . . . .

Rob And the price.

Gemma How much?

Lily Thirty quid.

Rob For fifteen minutes.

Lily Two quid a minute.

Rob Car drops her back.

Lily Another one comes along. Same routine, hey presto, sixty quid!

Rob Magic, Lils!

Lily Yeah, money's easy. You can earn it standing in a doorway, or flat on your back, or in the back of someone's car. You can use your body same as other people do – carpenters, mechanics, gardeners. You can go to work and earn it in a shop or you can work for yourself on the street corner or at home. Money's easy, same as everything's easy – once you know how . . . .

Gemma You didn't, you're pulling my leg aren't you?

Lily I was a little prossie for half an hour, now I'm Lily again and I'm having a really good time . . . .

Lily and **Rob** *inject each other; mutual bliss.* **Tar**, **Gemma** *and* **Sal** *all go off to separate space with tourniquet and syringe, and inject themselves. Music, The Only Ones, 'The Beast'.*

Scene Three

Richard, **Tar**.

Richard   Next month I'm going on a trip to South-East Asia. Cycling tour. Can you imagine Tar, cycling through Thailand, Bali, then on to Australia? Come with me Tar.

Tar *laughs*.

Richard   Why not?

Tar   I don't have any money.

Richard   I'll lend you some.

Tar (*shakes his head*)   You know I'd never give it back, even if I wanted to.

Richard   It doesn't matter, Tar, come with me anyway.

Tar   You just want me to leave the junk alone.

Richard   I would love you to come with me . . . .

Tar   But it is the junk isn't it?

Richard   It'll kill you. It is killing you. You're really boring these days.

Tar   So are you. (**Richard** *shakes his head*.) I don't have to go cycling off to South-East Asia to keep myself interesting, Richard.

Richard   I hope you find it just as interesting being dead as you have being alive.

Tar   I'm just trying to live my life, if that means I'll be dead in three years, that's fine by me. Send me a postcard Rich.

Scene Four

Vonny, **Gemma**, **Lily**.

Vonny   Everyone thinks that they're stronger than heroin. That's how it makes you feel. But there'll be deaths.

She gets really wound up.

Some of you are going to die.

Gemma   You know all about it, you've been through it, have you?

Vonny   No. There'll be deaths.

Lily   Yeah! You're all gonna die! Yeah! Live fast, die young, babe, before you get any older. Too fast to live, too young to die.

Scene Five

Sal, **Gemma**.

Through the following they mime giving professional blow-jobs and hand-jobs to customers. Music

Sal (*to audience*)   Me and Gemma have got this amazing job down the parlour – Dido's Health Parlour. It's nice and clean. It's safe, because you're on the premises and there's the other girls around, and the management don't want anything bad to happen or they lose their business.

Gemma (*to audience*)   I get three hundred quid a week some weeks, if I go for it. Fifteen years old, three hundred quid a week. I keep thinking I'd like to go back and show my parents. Not what I'm doing; not what I'm earning, either, 'cause they might guess. Just me. Just show them me, so they can see I'm doing all right.

Sal (*to audience*)   You get a better class of punter here. Lily has to take them as they come, straight off the street. Of course the management don't want people to get turned away so you can't pick and choose. You can't say, 'I don't fancy him, I'll have him instead'. But if someone asks you to do something kinky they send in Joe and he shows them the door. And the boss, Gordon, is really good too.

Gemma (*to audience*)   Only I can't go back. Not yet. I'd like to wait until I'm clean before that. I do too much, I know that. I keep meaning to ring them but . . . it does my head in. I just can't bear to talk to them these days. Even my mum. I miss her, but I can't talk to her. It'll come. I can wait. I mean, she's not gonna die tomorrow, right?

Sal (*to audience*)   It's a public service, really. After the bank-holiday you get this queue of men in the waiting room. If it wasn't for us they'd probably be out on the street hunting down young girls. Gemma and I have a joke about it. 'You on PPD today?'

Gemma (*to audience*)   Yeah, pervert prevention duty. (*Laughs and exits.*)

Scene Six

Lily, **Gemma**, **Sal**, **Rob**, **Tar**.

Lily *is standing on the sofa.*

Lily   I'm going to have a baby.

Gemma   Oh, my God! What are you going to do, what are you going to do?

Sal   Oh, Lils! Have you told a doctor yet? Has he given you a date?

Lily *glares at them.*

Lily   Listen Mrs Sister. You know what dead babies do. They come back and haunt. They're all over the place, I see 'em. Yeah – dead babies floating on the ceiling looking for their mums 'cause their mums had 'em scraped out and they never had a life . . . . I'm not gonna kill my baby. That's my baby. No one's gonna kill my baby.

Gemma   I didn't say kill it.

Lily   I said, I'm going to have a baby. I'm going to have it. A baby, a baby, Gems . . . .

Sal   You're on the game and you're a junkie, Lily. You ought to have an abortion.

Lily   Because you did? Are you telling me to kill my baby? Are you telling me . . . ?

Sal   You ought to have an abortion for the sake of the baby.

Lily   You want me to kill my baby? You wanna? You wanna kill it? Come on, come on, you kill it then, you do it now.

Sal   Your baby is a junkie. Your baby is inside you and it's full of junk, same as you. You want to give birth to a junkie? Is that what you want? Is that how much you love your bloody baby?

Lily   I'm a junkie? Are you telling me I'm a fucking junkie?

Sal   I'm telling you it's not fair to your baby to be pregnant with it while you're full of junk. What sort of a mother is that?

Lily *is walking up and down the room, poking herself on the chest and trying to find the words.*

Lily   I can give it up any time I want . . . .

Sal *laughs.* **Lily** *gives her a murderous look. Then* **Lily** *just turns round and walks out of the room.* **Sal** *sits back down and lights a fag.*

Gemma   Give us a fag, Sal.

Gemma *paces up and down the room trying to get calm.*

Sal   I think I'd better go.

Gemma   Don't go, don't go, it'll be all right, it'll be all right.

Next door **Lily** *has put The Cure, 'Lovecats' on.*

Gemma   See? She'll be okay.

Lily *comes back in. She is jiving about.* **Lily** *sings lines from 'Lovecats'. She starts to smile a big* **Lily** *smile. She sprawls like a tiger and puts her arms around* **Sal**.

Lily   Okay, Sal? Okay?

Sal   Yeah, I'm okay.

Lily   All right, Sal, mates again. Soul sisters . . . .

Sal   Yeah, soul sisters, eh?

Gemma   Yeah, yeah.

Lily   There's gonna be a baby, right? It's a fact. That's all there is to it. I'm gonna be a mother and you're gonna be it's mother and so's Gems and we're all gonna get clean and live the real life . . . . You're not gonna come round here junked up, you're not gonna give me junk when I'm pregnant . . . .

Gemma   No, right, no.

Even **Sal** *is nodding now.*

Lily   Everything's gotta change. You don't do junk when there's babies. It was good but now it's on to something else . . . . We'll have a baby in the house for Christmas.

All five are going to give up, now. They line up. 'Lovecats' continues under the following:

Rob   I'm gonna get a job and we're all going to move off the City Road where, let's face it, it's pretty squalid.

Lily   I'm coming off the game and I'm gonna grow veg in the garden and keep chickens 'n' everything.

Tar Me 'n' Rob are going to build a swing in the garden, just a little one for the baby. And we're doing the skips looking for a cot and all that baby stuff.

Gemma I'm thinking I'll stop doing tricks at work – I mean, full sex. It'd be up to me, you don't earn as much but you can still do all right.

Sal I was doubtful at first, but now I'm as keen as everyone. It's a real chance, me and Gems are already talking about having babies.

Lily Gems and me are going to knit! Imagine, us knitting! And the first thing – the big thing – we're all going to give up junk. The way I look at it, I had a love affair – but now it's over. Me and Junk, we've fallen out. It's just so right that we all get led out of it by a little baby. You know? Like baby Jesus. A baby is different isn't it?

All Yeah!

Scene Seven

Gemma, **Rob**, **Tar**, **Lily**.

Gemma (*to audience*)   Did I tell you, Lily turned blue the other day? Tar, Rob, Tar, Rob!

Rob *comes in, then* **Tar**. **Lily** *gets bluer and bluer.* **Tar** *pushes her back on the bed to press her heart.* **Rob** *pulls her upright, slaps her face. She twitches,* **Lily** *takes two little sips of air. They get her on her feet and* **Rob** *marches her round and round the room, her feet on his boots. She splutters alive into laughter . . .*

Lily Live fast, die young. (*She laughs at them for having worried.*) Live fast, die young . . .

Rob *is shattered,* **Gemma** *is shaken.*

Gemma (*to audience*)   The really awful thing was . . . I mean, the other awful thing was . . . . You see it was almost two weeks ago, that. No one has said anything. I know, I know, it's just a blob of jelly at this point, it isn't a person or anything. But I still keep thinking of how whatever it is went blue inside her as well. I was getting scared. Rob and Lily do so much. Every day. Tar and me – we have days off at least.

Scene Eight

Rob, **Lily**, **Gemma**, **Tar**, **Sal**.

Rob (*to audience*)   We had to get away for a bit. We had to leave it all behind, all the shit. The baby was the real magic spell and Lily was the witch who was making it. What does that make me? A magician I suppose. It's a bit like that. Me a dad. With my magic wand.

We were going away for a whole week. A whole week. Miles from anywhere; beautiful Welsh countryside, no people, no hassle, no problems. The cottage belongs to a friend of Wendy. Wendy's my mum. It was April, so it was free. We'd finished off the last of our junk before we set out, and we had just a tiny bit, a dab, just to get us to bed that night so in the morning we could start right from scratch. Personally, I was determined to have a real go at it.

I had a little package in my pocket that no one knew about, and I almost thought about throwing it away but I didn't want to muck things up. I'm lousy at that coming down bit. You have to find the best way of going about things. That little package was right for me.

They enter the countryside with cigarettes, joints, cans of Special Brew. They look very happy and pleased with themselves.

We went for a walk, over the hill and down into the valley beyond.

Walk music begins. It gets louder and louder as their cold-turkey gets worse and worse. Light gets brighter and brighter on them, so they are more and more exposed, more uncomfortable, more ugly. They sustain the walk as long as possible. They get more and more tired as they go, as none of them has had any exercise for so long. **Lily** *stops, they all stop. They all look shifty and jaded, completely unsuited to the environment they are in. Music builds to its climax.* **Lily** *cracks first.*

Lily   Fuck this! Fuck this!

Stillness. Silence.

Gemma (*intensely*)   God I didn't expect to feel this bad.

They look at each other. **Gemma** *and* **Tar** *are feeling terrible,* **Rob** *laughs,* **Sal** *catches* **Rob**'s *eye,* **Lily** *looks very unwell. She turns round and stomps back to the cottage. They all turn round to follow* **Lily** *– but not before* **Sal** *and* **Rob** *smirk at each other.*

Rob (*to audience*)   Well, what did they expect? We got back to the cottage and we built a big fire to try and make it cosy and we did what we could to try and keep the heebie jeebies away.

Tar   I wanna get some booze.

Gemma   You'll only get a hangover, and then what about tomorrow.

Tar   I need it, I need it Gems, you don't understand.

Tar *exits.*

Sal   You can't make coming down feel good, you just have to go through it.

Rob   Yeah, it'll be easier tomorrow.

Sal *and* **Rob** *catch eyes.* **Gemma** *runs out to vomit,* **Sal** *follows her.* **Lily** *notices* **Rob** *is not showing signs of coming down.*

Lily   Gimmee.

Rob   What do you mean Lils?

Lily   Gimmee. Give me some.

Rob   What about the baby?

Lily   Please, please.

Rob *gives some junk to* **Lily** *who snorts it.*

Lily *and* **Rob** *lie back and they relax.* **Gemma** *is making a
terrible noise outside with violent stomach cramps.* **Gemma** *enters
and instantly sees what they are doing.*

Gemma   You've had some. (*To* **Rob**.) Did you bring it?
Did you give it to her? What about the baby, Lily? Lily?
The baby. Uh? Lily. What about your baby, Lily? Lily, the
baby. What about your baby, Lily? Lily, the baby. YOUR
baby. Lily, Lily, the BABY. What about YOUR BABY?
Murderer! You murderer! I'd have done it if just one of you
bastards had hung out with me. Just give me some, just give
me some will you.

Rob *gives* **Gemma** *some junk.*

Rob (*to audience*)   I couldn't say no could I? I thought, This
is no fun. We never even stayed a second night in Wendy's
cottage.

Scene Nine

Gemma, **Tar**.

Back in their Bristol squat. **Tar** *and* **Gemma** *are very separate.*

Gemma   You really hitch-hiked all the way back?

Tar   I should have taken a bit with me.

Gemma   Rob did.

Tar   I thought so.

Gemma   Why didn't you ask him, instead of hitching all
the way back?

Tar   I don't know. Don't get at me. How do you think I
feel about it?

Gemma   It doesn't matter anyway.

Tar Look, I only went along with it because the rest of you were so keen. I cleared off because I didn't want to tempt you. Live fast, die young, you know Gems . . . .

Gemma You don't really think like that.

Tar You don't know anything about it when you're dead.

Gemma Yeah, but no more junk for deadies.
You never even do anything to that sodding dandelion any more.

Tar *puts his arms round her. She just weeps. Music, The Buzzcocks, 'Ever Fallen in Love With Someone' starts.*

I just want the old Tar back, the one I used to know.

She buries her head against his stomach.

I love you.

Tar I've been waiting for you to say that all these years, I love you too.

Gemma Dandelion, dandelion, Tar.

The Buzzcocks, 'Ever Fallen in Love With Someone' fades out quickly.

Scene Ten

Policeman, **Policewoman**, **Tar**, **Gemma**.

Police siren goes off, very loudly. Blue light erupts in centre of the stage. **Policeman** *and* **Policewoman** *enter. They grab* **Gemma** *and* **Tar**. *They are forcibly placed on either side of the stage, maximum distance between them. The policeman holds a plastic bag. Music climaxes, louder.*

Policeman Is this yours, David?

Tar Yeah, that's mine, it's all mine.

Policeman I arrest you under suspicion of being in possession of Class A drugs, and holding Class A drugs for the purpose of sale to person or persons unknown. I must warn you . . . .

Tar *keeps glancing at the door where* **Gemma** *might be.*

Tar   Where's Gemma, where's Gemma? Gemma, Gemma!

He is struggling to get through the door. The **Policeman** *grabs him and pins him to the wall, feet off the ground.*

Gemma   I'm all right, Tar, I'm okay . . . .

Policewoman   Shut your gob!

Tar   You could have told me she was okay, it wouldn't have done you any harm.

Policeman   Stupid little toe-rag.

Tar *yells out at the top of his lungs.*

Tar   The stuff's mine, Gems, okay.

The woman on the other side of the door screams:

Policewoman   Shut his fucking mouf!

Policeman   Clever little git, aren't you.

They lead **Gemma** *out into the hall.* **Tar** *and* **Gemma** *are put into the police car. Sound of the siren again.*

Scene Eleven

Tar, **Steve**.

The detox centre. **Tar** *sits with others.*

Tar (*to audience*)   Nah, it's not prison. My case doesn't come up for another three months. This is the detox centre in Weston-Super-Mare. The first thing that happened when I came here, they got all the new intake together and told us what was what. There were about ten of us sitting around, and this hippie-looking bloke – I thought he was one of us at first – suddenly started talking.

Steve   No one's keeping you here. Anytime you feel you've had enough, there's the door. But while you do stay here, no drugs of any kind are allowed. Not even aspirin.

Tar *laughs nervously.* **Steve** *smiles.*

Not even hash, I like a smoke and if I have to go without it, so can you. If any of you feel you can't do it, you'd be better to go now. Really. Go now and you can come back another time. Wait until you get caught – you've blown it forever. If you get caught taking drugs here, you'll never come back again.

Scene Twelve

Gemma, **Tar**.

Gemma (*to audience*)   I write to him every day. I was looking at a letter he wrote to me the other day and those words on the bottom he writes.

Tar   Dandelion, I love you.

Gemma   And I thought that was magic.

Gemma/Tar   Loving someone. It's not you and it's not them. It's not in you it's between you. It's bigger and stronger than you are.

Tar   Dandelion.

Gemma   Dandelion.

Tar   That's what I believe in. It's the only thing can help me now.

Scene Thirteen

Steve, **Tar**.

Tar *is suffering badly from withdrawal.*

Steve   Come on Tar, you can do it, just another few days and you'll be clean.

Tar   All I want is junk. I want to leave.

Steve *sits and watches* **Tar** *for a bit.*

Steve   Do you want something to help you?

Tar   What do you mean?

Steve   I can't give you heroin, but I have some methadone for severe cases. I can get you a prescription. (*He holds out a key.*) This is the key to the medicine cabinet. You can have it in two minutes if you like.

Tar   Why methadone?

Steve   Heroin is illegal and methadone isn't.

Tar   Please, yeah, anything.

Steve   Okay, I'll go and get it, you pack your bag.

Tar   What?

Steve   If you want some you can have it, but you have to leave. (*He holds out the key.*) Two minutes, Tar.

Tar *stares at the key, then he stares at* **Steve**.

Steve *smiles.*

Tar   Just . . . fuck off.

Steve *nods respectfully and leaves.* **Tar** *gets up and walks around. Music, he opens up, he breathes fully, he is healthy and well.*

Tar (*to audience*)   I was out in the grounds the other day. I came across this bush full of red berries and it was just blazing. And the air smelt of leaves and soil. The colour was

so bright it hurt my eyes. I don't mean like coming down,
when bright colours are really unpleasant. I'm clean now. It
was just a blaze of red, and I felt I was looking at something
for the first time in three years. I thought, All that time the
junk has been between me and the world around me, like a
fat cushion you can't see through or hear through or touch
through. It's like three years that never were.

Scene Fourteen

Gemma, **Rob**, **Tar**, **Sal**, **Lily**.

Tar *arrives back to the following scene:* **Lily** *is sitting in the upstage,
centre of the room, she glows and is surrounded by cushions. She is
breast-feeding a very small baby. Her presence, though quiet and still,
dominates the room.* **Gemma** *is held in a moment of silent rapture
just before embracing* **Tar**. **Sal** *looks on from the side, coolly
surveying, judging* **Tar**. **Rob** *slaps him on the back – and the place
explodes into cacophony.*

Gemma   Tar, Tar, I've missed you sooo much.

Rob   All right, Tar?

Tar   Yeah mate.

Sal   Alllriiiight!

Tar   Yeah. (*Laughs.*)

Gemma *takes* **Tar** *to* **Lily**.

Gemma   Meet Sonny, the baby.

Tar   Oh yeah!

Tar *holds the baby.*

Lily   Isn't he beautiful! Hey, Tar, you look different.

Tar *offers Lambrusco to everyone. No one is interested.* **Gemma**
puts on The Clash, 'I'm Not Down' for him. They dance and yell.

Lily injects a vein very close to her breast. **Rob** *holds the baby.* **Lily** *gets up and kicks the cassette player. The music stops.*

Lily Brainwashed. Yeah, what a drag. They took him off one drug and put him on another. They done a good job on you mate . . . .

Sal Leave him alone, he's doing all right.

Lily Yeah, they put him in prison all right. They locked you up inside your own head and then they gave you the key and how did you get out of that jail? They made you your own jailer, it's cheaper for 'em that way . . . .

Tar You can think what you want, Lily. You're on junk and I'm not.

Tar *gets up and goes outside.* **Gemma***'s head drops slightly, she follows. Sharp cut to thudding sound of party.* **Rob** *injets himself on a sofa.* **Tar** *enters the room and pauses. He picks up a tin with junk in. He looks at* **Rob** *for approval.* **Rob** *shrugs.* **Tar** *pours some junk on to a piece of foil and chases it.* **Lily** *comes in and looks at* **Tar***. She has the baby with her. She sees what* **Tar** *has done and looks at him in disgust.*

Tar (*to* **Lily** *defensively*) Gemma did some.

Lily Oh that's all right then. (*To* **Rob**.) You prat.

Rob He asked me what was I supposed to do?

Sal Oh leave him alone Lily, for God's sake, it's supposed to be a party.

Lily Look at him he's practically gauching out . . . .

Tar I only had a chase, I didn't use a needle.

Sal You're making too much of it, Lily, it's his party.

Tar It doesn't mean I haven't given up.

Sal Oh god!

Lily Oh, yeah, you take the stuff but you've still given up, sure . . . .

Tar This is a party. Anyway, Gemma did some tonight. She told me. She asked me if it was okay.

Lily And you said yes.

Tar *smiles. Pause.*

Tar Don't tell her, will you, Lily? It won't do her any good, you won't be doing her any favours.

Lily Yeah, you want me to play your game. How are you going to feel about this tomorrow?

Tar I expect I'll think I fancied some junk, Lily.

Lily You've really buggered it up for both of you.

Enter **Gemma**.

Tar Dandelion, I love you.

Music, The Buzzcocks, 'Everybody's Happy Nowadays'.

Scene Fifteen

Richard, **Tar**.

Richard's *house*.

Richard (*to audience*) Tar came to see me. He helped me move into my new house in Reading, I asked him if he was clean. I didn't want any needles in the house. He seemed slightly offended when I asked him. He was his usual shifty self. I mean, that's usual for him since he got on to junk. He'd lost that open look he used to have about him quite early on . . . It was funny. I hadn't actually liked him for years. But I kept getting little glimpses. He'd look at me shyly out of the corner of his eye, and I'd think the old Tar was still in there somewhere.

Suddenly **Tar** *gets up and pulls his coat on.*

Where are you off to?

Tar   I'm going back.

Richard   What for?

Tar *shrugs. His eyes drift across the floor.*

Tar   I need to go back. Can you lend me the bus fare? I've left myself with no money.

Richard   Tar, I'm sorry. Isn't there anything else I can do?

Tar   No, no, I just have to get back.

Richard   Why?

Tar   I'm coming down, I'm doing cold-turkey, but I can't go through with it. I want to go back and get some junk.

Richard   Why didn't you just say?

Tar   I didn't want to tell you I was coming down. Look. (*Spreads hands open.*) I'll only hitch home if you don't. I can't do it, Richard, I'm sorry, I can't do it. Not this time. I'd better go.

Richard   Wait. Tar, can't I help you some other way?

Tar   Look at me, look at me Richard. (*Shakes **Richard** by the shoulder.*)

Richard *looks at him.*

I'm just a junkie. I'm just a junkie and I just want to get back and get on with . . . .

Begins to cry. Strength leaves him and he falls to his knees. **Richard** *cradles him in his arms.*

I'm just a junkie, I'm just a junkie, I'm just a junkie, I'm just a junkie, I'm just a junkie.

Richard (*to audience*)   I gave him his bus fare.

Music, The Flying Lizards, 'Money'.

Scene Sixteen

Gemma, **Lily**, **Rob**, **Tar**.

Setting changes to **Gemma** *and* **Tar**'s *squat.* **Gemma** *sits on a pallet covered in a rug. She looks at a pregnancy tester, which is sat on top of an electric fire. A door is upstage, centre, which everyone enters and exits through.*

Gemma (*to audience, in a nightdress*)   We live in our own place now. Lily and Rob and Sunny the baby live two streets away. I don't know why I love him so much. It always used to be the other way round, him loving me more. I don't understand myself, because he's a bastard now, really. He lies, he cheats. He pinches my money. Just helps himself out of my purse. He nicks our stash, and doesn't come back till he's finished it. Then his eyes sort of swivel about and he tells me he loves me. I don't know if it's true any more. I want to have Tar's baby. Now that's really stupid, isn't it?

There is a very loud pounding on the door. **Tar** *awakens and points frantically at the door.* **Gemma** *gets up and opens it.*

Lily (*hushed and in a dressing gown at the street door*)   Please, please, please.

Lily *is moaning and weeping. She cannot speak, she cannot walk, she has one hand on her throat.*

Gemma   God . . . .

Tar *puts her on the sofa.* **Gemma** *takes the baby.* **Lily** *throws up over the side of the sofa.*

Gemma (*to audience*)   I got the story eventually, it was a punter. He came up and got her to undress and then asked her to do something she didn't want to do. When she said no, he grabbed a pair of her old tights and he put them round her neck and pulled them tight, really tight. He really pulled them tight.

Simultaneously noise of police sirens in the distance. Pounding on the door. **Sunny** *the baby is screaming.* **Gemma** *opens the door.* **Rob** *stands there, his head is bleeding.*

Lily   You stupid idiot, you rang the police, the house is full of needles, scales, heroin, everything, you stupid . . . .

Rob   That bloke who came in tried to kill you Lils.

Gemma *looks at the pregnancy tester.*

Gemma (*shouts*)   I *am* pregnant.

Blackout. Music, The Buzzcocks, 'Everybody's Happy Nowadays'.

Scene Seventeen

Gemma, **Lily**.

Gemma *checks outside the door, then comes down to the pallet and sits to address the audience.*

Gemma   I didn't tell Tar about me being pregnant. I knew what he'd say. He'd want me to have it. He keeps saying we should have a baby like Rob and Lily. It's stupid. We're both junkies. But the really awful thing is – I want to have it, too. I lay in bed and I thought for a long, long time. About Tar. About Lily and Rob and Sunny. You look in that baby's eyes – he's *full* of it – junk, I mean. He must get it through the milk. She even rubs a few grains on his gums if he's playing up. He's a junkie, he's been a junkie all his little life, he was a junkie even before he was born.
What was scaring me was, that little blob of jelly inside me seemed like the only thing worth anything I had in the whole world.

Lily *walks in carrying a mug of tea and holding* **Sunny**, *interrupting* **Gemma**'s *address to the audience.* **Lily** *is weak and exhausted.*

Lily   Hi.

Gemma (*startled*)   Hi.

Lily Yeah. He won't sleep, I'm looking for his dodee. (*She yawns and smiles.*)

Gemma Let me hold him for a bit. I wanna have one.

Lily Yeah, you will one day, Gems, you deserve it.

Gemma How's your neck?

Lily It hurts.

Lily *smiles,* **Gemma** *smiles back at her.*

Gemma I think he's filled his nappy.

Lily I'll finish my tea first. He might do some more . . . .

Gemma I'll do it.

Lily Nah, I'll do it.

Lily *begins to doze.* **Gemma** *picks up* **Sunny***, puts him down on the floor and undoes his nappy. She wipes him clean and lets him try to suck her nose.* **Lily** *wakes and sees what* **Gemma** *is doing.* **Lily** *is dangerous again.*

Lily You didn't have to do that, Gems.

Gemma You fell asleep.

Lily *brushes past* **Gemma** *and picks up* **Sunny***. She looks at* **Gemma** *as if she doesn't know who she is.*

Lily No one's ever gonna take my baby off me.

Gemma I never said that, I never said that.

Lily No one's ever gonna.

Lily *turns away with the baby, she is going to cry. She gives* **Gemma** *a little glance over her shoulder, her face is scared. She cradles her head against* **Sunny** *and rubs her cheek into him, and kisses him and loves him.*

He's a lovely baby, Gems.

She is just trying to be normal, but it isn't normal. She stands there staring at **Gemma***. Her eyes are full of tears.* **Gemma** *reaches out* *to hold her but she just shakes her head, a stiff little shake. She sits down on the settee.* **Gemma** *cannot move.* **Gemma** *doesn't know what to do, she thinks she might suddenly jump up and stab her or something.*

I've had it, Gems, I'm going to bed.

Gemma   Okay, Lil.

She gets up and has to walk past **Gemma** *on her way to the door.* **Gemma** *has to force herself not to move back away from her.*

Lily   It'll be all right, Gems.

Gemma   I know, Lily.

Lily   Night.

Gemma   Night.

Lily *turns at the door and gives* **Gemma** *a big warm smile, and that scared little look again. After a pause* **Gemma** *grabs the rug off the pallet and wraps it round herself and lets herself out of the front door. She goes very quickly round the corner. She gets to the telephone booth and dials 999.*

Police please.

Cast clears the stage of every piece of furniture with dramatic speed. Music, Haircut 100, 'Boy Meets Girl'.

Scene Eighteen

Vonny, **Gemma**, **Mrs Brogan** (*on phone*).

On an empty stage, only the phone box remains.

Vonny (*to audience*)   I'm at college now. On Wednesdays we play badminton, me and my bloke John. I stayed over at his place. When I got back today, one of the neighbours said this punk type had been hanging about on my doorstep for hours and hours. One of the really scabby ones. It was six in the evening before I discovered the note. She must have

pushed it through my letterbox, but there's a little piece of
carpet I use as a mat and sometimes it rucks up and letters
get stuck underneath it. 'I can't wait any longer, I'm going
to the hospital to try and get them to admit me. Gemma.'
I hadn't seen her for ages. It got worse and worse round
there, full of brain-dead zombies. I used to go round and
nag her about it quite often. She was boasting about it all
the time – being on the game, using needles.
I ran out and jumped in the car and drove straight there.

Lights come up on **Gemma**. *She is lying centre stage in a hospital
bed. She has been wheeled on during* **Vonny***'s speech.*

Gemma, it's Vonny.

Gemma Hello.

Vonny (*to audience*) She looked like death. As I listened to
her story, I kept thinking, she's eighteen and I'm twenty-
four, but she's so much older than I am. She's an addict,
she's fallen in love, she's slept with dozens of men, she's
pregnant. She was only eighteen but I felt like I was listening
to an old, old woman telling me stories about things that
had happened to her as a young girl.
Give me your parent's number, Gemma. Let's try that first.

Gemma I can't.

Vonny It's out of your hands, Gemma. Just say the
number.

Gemma *covers her face with her hands.*

Gemma 0232 671429

Vonny (*to audience*) She'd remembered it after all these
years.

Vonny *goes to the phone box and dials the number.* **Mrs Brogan**
enters.

Mrs Brogan Hello.

Vonny Mrs Brogan?

Mrs Brogan Yes.

Vonny It's about your daughter, Gemma.

Scene Nineteem

Mrs. Brogan, **Gemma**.

Gemma *still in hospital bed.*

Mrs Brogan (*to audience*)   My first thought was, My God, she looks like my mother. Despite everything, I still thought of her as a fourteen-year-old girl. But she looked like my mother, my own mother. An old woman. I wanted to make it as normal as possible for her, talk about home and ask her what she'd done, although how on earth we could talk about what she'd done in those years I don't know. I didn't want to cry and I knew that I shouldn't but I thought of all the things I'd missed and I couldn't help it, I couldn't get half of what I'd planned on saying out, I just started to weep. And she was crying too. I knew it was all right when she started to cry. The tears said everything for us.

Gemma   I want to come home, Mum, can I come home, Mum, please . . . ?

Mrs Brogan   Yes, Yes. (*They hold one another and cry.*)

Scene Twenty

Tar, **Gemma**.

On a train to Minely, **Tar** *has just been released from prison.*

Tar (*to audience*)   After the raid I did my time. I've been clean for over three months now, I may not have done it myself out of choice, but I'm clean now and that's the important thing. Gemma, she did her cold-turkey at home and that was that. With my history you can't rush it. You have to be positive before you can do anything, like the

doctor said. Anyway, it's something to build on.
The last time I saw Gems, she was as big as a house. She got
bigger and bigger every time she came to see me. And now
she's bringing our baby, Oona.

Tar *gets down from the train. Music, The Cure, 'Boys Don't Cry'.*
He is pale and grey after being locked up so long. He has a small bag.
Gemma *holds* **Oona**. **Gemma** *and* **Tar** *come towards each*
other soberly. **Gemma** *gives him a big, long, slow, hard hug.*
Gemma *then gives* **Tar** *the baby.* **Gemma** *then looks again at*
Tar *and takes back the baby. She exits towards stage left and freezes.*
Music stops.

Tar *(to audience)*   Love is forever!
Yeah, well I don't believe that any more. Being an addict . . .
now that's forever.
It was a love story. Me, Gemma and Junk.

Blackout.

End.

Songs used in the Oxford Stage Company production of *Junk*.

'Girls Just Wanna Have Fun' – Cyndi Lauper
'I'm Not Down' – The Clash
'Waltzin' Black' – The Stranglers
'Ever Fallen In Love With Someone' – The Buzzcocks
'Hit Me With Your Rhythm Stick' – Ian Dury and the Blockheads
'Another Girl, Another Planet' – The Only Ones
'Skin Up For Jesus' – Cleaning Jesus
'Reggae' – Karl James
'Golden Brown' – The Stranglers
'Weekend' – Karl James
'Tar's Hit' – Karl James
'Blue Monday' – New Order
'The Clangers' – Vernon Elliott
'The Beast' – The Only Ones
'Brothel' – Karl James
'Lovecats' – The Cure
'Awful' – Karl James
'The Walk' – Karl James
'Thud' – Karl James
'Everybody's Happy Nowadays' – The Buzzcocks
'Money' – The Flying Lizards
'Boy Meets Girl' – Haircut 100
'Boys Don't Cry' – The Cure